THE STORY OF
TAYLOR
SWIFT

An Inspiring Biography for Young Readers

— Written by —   —Illustrated by—

Rachelle Burk   **Marta Dorado**

callisto
publishing
an imprint of Sourcebooks

To Cara, Alana, and David—
thank you for the music!

CONTENTS

CHAPTER 1

A STAR IS BORN

◎ **Meet Taylor Swift** ◎

Imagine how Taylor Swift felt when she heard her name announced at the 2009 Country Music Association Awards in Nashville, Tennessee.

"And the award for Entertainer of the Year goes to...Taylor Swift!"

She felt as if she was in a dream! Taylor was only 19 years old, and she was the youngest person ever to win this big award.

When she walked onstage to accept the award, Taylor knew it wasn't just her talent that had brought her here. She owed her success to her dedicated fans, her loving family, and the musical artists who **inspired** her.

Taylor is famous for writing songs about her own life and feelings. She was a preteen when she started writing music. Many young girls felt as if her songs were also about their own lives. As Taylor grew up, her fans grew up with her.

WHERE?

PENNSYLVANIA

WEST READING

New people started to love her music, too. In a few years, Taylor became one of the most famous **singer-songwriters** ever.

But Taylor isn't famous just for her music. Her fans look up to her. She gives money to important causes and helps fans in need. She stands up for things she believes in, such as women's rights, gun control, and fair pay for musicians. Taylor has won many awards. But more important, she's won a lot of hearts. She's a true role model for people all around the world.

◎ Taylor's World ◎

Taylor Alison Swift was born in
West Reading, Pennsylvania, on
December 13, 1989. She lived with
her parents, Andrea and Scott Swift,
and her younger brother, Austin.
Taylor's family was really into music.
Her parents named her after their
favorite singer-songwriter, James Taylor. He is
a **pop** rock artist who sang popular songs such
as "You've Got a Friend" and "Country Road."

JUMP –IN THE– THINK TANK

Everyone has a dream. What is yours? How can you work to achieve it?

The Swifts (1996)

Her grandmother Marjorie Finlay was an **opera** singer. She was a big inspiration for Taylor.

When Taylor was growing up, most of her classmates sang along to pop music by artists such as Britney Spears and the Backstreet Boys. Some kids listened to rap music by artists such as Jay-Z or Queen Latifah. Others preferred rock music played with drums and electric guitars.

But Taylor liked the **country music** that came out of Nashville, Tennessee. Artists such as Dolly Parton, Garth Brooks, and Shania Twain wrote songs that told stories. Country music first became

popular in southern and southwestern states. It was often played with instruments such as guitars, banjos, and fiddles. The **lyrics** talked about things like love, work, and family.

Although country music was less popular where Taylor lived, Taylor dreamed of becoming a country music star. She knew it wouldn't be easy. But Taylor was talented and willing to work hard.

> " Maybe you're **not meant to fit in.** Maybe you're supposed to **stand out.** "

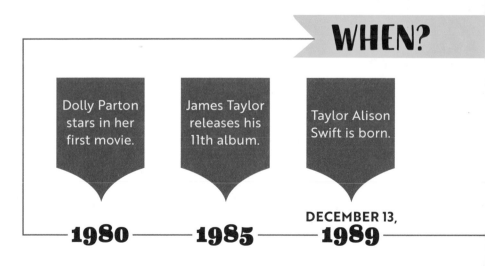

WHEN?

Dolly Parton stars in her first movie.

James Taylor releases his 11th album.

Taylor Alison Swift is born.

1980 — 1985 — DECEMBER 13, 1989

CHAPTER 2

THE EARLY YEARS

Growing Up

Taylor grew up in a happy family. Her dad, Scott, worked in finance. Her mom, Andrea, stayed home to raise Taylor and her brother, Austin. Austin is two years younger.

Taylor's family wanted to live in a peaceful, quiet place. They bought a Christmas tree farm an hour away from Philadelphia, Pennsylvania. Taylor loved Christmas, and the farm kept her in the Christmas spirit all year long. She loved living there. She played with her brother, rode horses, and even competed in horse shows. She also liked to bake and to spend summers at the Jersey Shore.

MYTH	&	FACT
Country music has been around since the United States became a country.		Country music began in the 1920s.

Taylor's biggest passion was music, especially country music. She enjoyed singing along to her favorite songs. Her parents saw her talent. When she was nine years old, they let her take acting and voice lessons in New York City. It was about two hours away from where Taylor lived.

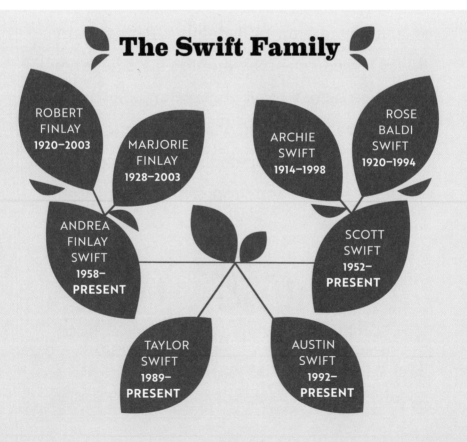

The Swift Family

ROBERT
FINLAY
1920–2003

MARJORIE
FINLAY
1928–2003

ARCHIE
SWIFT
1914–1998

ROSE
BALDI
SWIFT
1920–1994

ANDREA
FINLAY
SWIFT
1958–
PRESENT

SCOTT
SWIFT
1952–
PRESENT

TAYLOR
SWIFT
1989–
PRESENT

AUSTIN
SWIFT
1992–
PRESENT

She even joined a local theater group. She adored being onstage!

Taylor had other talents, too. She did well in creative writing. She loved words as much as she loved music. She wrote poetry and stories. She filled diaries with her thoughts and feelings. In fourth grade, she won a poetry contest with a poem called "A Monster in My Closet." In middle school, she wrote a novel titled *A Girl Named Girl* during summer vacation. Her ability to tell stories helped her grow into a great songwriter.

◎ A Love of Music ◎

Taylor first fell in love with country music at the age of six, when she listened to an **album** by LeAnn Rimes, a 13-year-old country music star. Taylor started listening to other country artists like Faith Hill, Shania Twain, and the Dixie Chicks (now known as the Chicks). She liked their music and she connected with the stories in their song lyrics. Taylor wanted to be just like her country music heroes. It would take hard work and practice, but that did not bother her. She liked a challenge.

When Taylor turned 12, she began taking guitar lessons. She practiced until her fingers were sore. At first, she only knew how to play three **chords**, but she used them to write her first song. It was called "Lucky You," and it was about a girl who wasn't afraid to be different.

Like the girl in her song, Taylor was different from the other kids in middle school. Unlike the

girl in her song, Taylor didn't want to be different. Girls teased her because she listened to country music. They also said mean things about the way she looked. Taylor tried to fit in by playing sports, but she wasn't very good at any of them. She felt like she didn't belong.

But Taylor had a special gift. When she was sad and lonely, she turned her feelings into song lyrics.

JUMP -IN THE- THINK TANK

When she was sad or lonely, Taylor wrote music to feel better. What do you do to help yourself feel better?

WHERE?

NEW YORK

PENNSYLVANIA

NEW YORK CITY

WEST READING

Writing music made her feel better. The more songs she wrote, the more she dreamed of going to Nashville. Her favorite country music stars started their **careers** in Nashville. Taylor couldn't wait for a chance to go.

WHEN?

1996	1999	2001
LeAnn Rimes's first album comes out.	Taylor begins voice and acting lessons.	Taylor begins playing guitar and writing music.

CHAPTER 3

A BIG MOVE

◎ Welcome to Nashville

Nashville is not only the capital of Tennessee—it's also the country music capital of the world. Country music legends like Dolly Parton, Kenny Chesney, and Faith Hill all started their music careers there.

Music has always been an important part of Nashville. Its nickname is "Music City." Nashville is home to famous music halls like the Opry House and the Ryman Auditorium, and many **studios** where musicians record their songs.

When Taylor was in sixth grade, she begged her parents to take her to Nashville. Her mother finally said yes, and they planned the trip for spring break. Nashville was a two-and-a-half-hour flight from Philadelphia, Pennsylvania. Before they left, Taylor sang songs by Dolly

Parton and the Dixie Chicks, and recorded them onto special **CDs**.

When they got to Nashville, Taylor went to a place called Music Row. It's a historic part of the city with **record labels**, recording studios, radio stations, and places where musicians **perform**. Taylor's mom and brother went along with Taylor to the offices of record labels. She gave them her CD in the hope that they would hear her music and give her a record deal. Taylor waited for her phone to ring. But none of the record labels called. They did not take a child from Pennsylvania seriously.

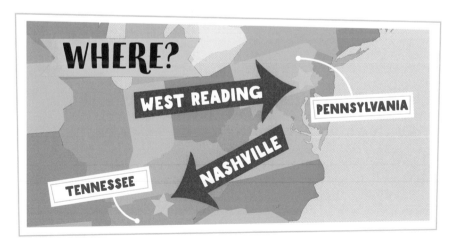

Taylor was disappointed, but she wouldn't give up. She knew that big dreams take time.

◎ A New Home ◎

Back in Pennsylvania, Taylor kept writing songs and performing. Then she had an idea. The best way for many people to notice her would be to sing the national anthem at sports games. She sent videos of herself singing to sports team managers. It worked! At age 12, Taylor stood in front of thousands of people at a Philadelphia 76ers basketball game and sang "The Star-Spangled Banner." The crowd cheered.

Taylor's family believed in her. They agreed that she needed to be in Nashville if she wanted a country music career. In 2004, the Swift family moved to Hendersonville, Tennessee, a short distance from Nashville. Taylor liked her new school, Hendersonville High. She made friends there. She met her best friend, Abigail Anderson, in English class. Taylor went to parties and started to go on dates. Now she felt inspired to write songs about joy and love rather than songs about being sad and lonely.

Taylor kept visiting record labels in Nashville. Finally, a music company called Sony/ATV was impressed by her lyrics. They offered her a **contract** as a songwriter.

At age 14, Taylor was the youngest songwriter they had ever signed. She wanted to be treated like an adult, so she was always polite and brought her best song ideas to work. She began working with a songwriter named Liz Rose. Liz was impressed by Taylor. They met every week after school to write songs together. Liz helped Taylor become a better writer and turn her ideas into songs.

> Believe in everything you do.
> ## Believe in your mistakes
> and grow from them.

WHEN?

Taylor visits Nashville for the first time.	Taylor sings the national anthem at a basketball game.	The Swift family moves to Tennessee.	Taylor becomes a songwriter for Sony.
2001	**2002**	**2004**	**2004**

CHAPTER 4

NEW

OPPORTUNITIES

The Bluebird Cafe

At Sony, Taylor wrote some songs for other country singers. But mostly her lyrics told her own story as a teenage girl. She wrote about following her dreams, friendships, boys she liked, and even about the love between her elderly neighbors.

Sony had hired her as a songwriter, not a singer. But she got to sing her songs in small clubs around Nashville. She made a new CD of songs she wrote herself and continued to share it with record labels.

MYTH FACT

MYTH: Musicians always release all the songs on an album at once.

FACT: Musicians often release one to two songs, called singles, a few months before a full album to get fans excited.

WHERE?

MUSIC ROW

NASHVILLE

TENNESSEE

One night, Taylor sang at the Bluebird Cafe, a place where new songwriters get to perform their own music. Many country music stars have been discovered there. That night, Scott Borchetta was in the audience. He was a famous **music producer**. He thought Taylor was special and offered her a recording contract. She was the first artist he signed to his new label, Big Machine Records. Taylor left Sony, feeling thankful for everything she learned there. Her dream was finally coming true!

In 2006, Taylor recorded her first song with Big Machine. It was called "Tim McGraw."

It told the story of a boyfriend who had moved away. She sang about everything she wanted him to remember, such as dancing to a song by the real country music singer Tim McGraw.

To **promote** her new song, Taylor and her mom traveled to different cities for six months. Taylor performed her song for radio stations. Sometimes they stayed in hotels. Other times they slept in the car. Taylor was determined to succeed. Her song became a huge hit!

◎ The First Album ◎

As Taylor's singing career grew, she became too busy to go to a regular high school. With her parents' help, she decided to **homeschool**. She could learn from home and have time to record songs and go on **tour**. Every day became a mix of learning and making music. She did her schoolwork in airports, between performances, and on her bedroom floor. Although she missed her social life at school, she always made time for her best friend, Abigail.

Taylor loved working with Big Machine, her new record label. Her manager, Scott, encouraged her to be creative and work on her own music. She released her first album in October 2006, when she was 16 years old. It was called *Taylor Swift*. Taylor wrote or helped write every song on the album. "Tim McGraw" was a big hit, but it wasn't the only one.

Taylor wrote "Our Song" when she was in the ninth grade. It was about a couple who made a special song from the sounds of all the fun things they did together. "Teardrops on My Guitar" was about a girl who liked a boy, but the boy saw her only as a friend.

These songs and many others were about Taylor's real life and experiences, and fans connected with her lyrics. The album quickly moved up the **Billboard charts**. It became the number one country album, and even a top pop album!

JUMP
—IN THE—
THINK TANK

Taylor was homeschooled to manage her busy schedule. What would you miss most if you couldn't go to your school?

WHEN?

Taylor signs with Big Machine Records.

Taylor begins to homeschool

Taylor releases her first album, *Taylor Swift.*

2005 — **2006** — **2006**

CHAPTER 5
DREAMS COME TRUE

◎ A Rising Star ◎

Taylor's first album sold more than a million copies in the first year it was released. It was so successful that Taylor was invited to go on tour with famous country singers such as George Strait, Ronnie Milsap, and Brad Paisley. She gained more fans along the way.

The next year, Tim McGraw and Faith Hill asked Taylor to join them on their **concert** tour. Taylor was so excited! Tim had inspired her first hit song. Faith was one of her biggest role models. They taught Taylor a lot about touring and performing onstage.

In November 2008, Taylor released her second album. It was called *Fearless*. Taylor was now 18 years old, so this album was all about her older teenage life and relationships. Just before she finished recording, the boy she was dating broke up with her. She wrote a song about the breakup.

JUMP
–IN THE–
THINK
TANK

For Taylor, success meant being a music star. In what way would you like to be successful?

"Forever and Always" was done just in time to add it to the album. *Fearless* had other hit songs like "Love Story," "White Horse," and "You Belong with Me." In 2009, it was the top-selling album in America. Taylor won four **Grammy** awards for it. She toured six countries and even appeared on the TV show *Saturday Night Live* twice that year, once as the musical guest and once as the host. Everyone was talking about Taylor Swift!

GRAMMY AWARDS
FEMALE COUNTRY VOCAL PERFORMANCE
White Horse — TAYLOR SWIFT

But then something happened that wasn't very nice. At a **music video** awards show, Taylor won the award for Best Female Video. A famous rapper and producer grabbed her microphone and interrupted her speech. He thought someone else should have won. Taylor kept a smile on her face but was upset and embarrassed. Not everyone was kind or supportive.

Taylor the Storyteller

As Taylor's music grew more popular, her fans began to call themselves by the name "Swifties." They related to the personal stories in Taylor's lyrics. Even people who didn't usually listen to country music enjoyed her songs.

Soon Taylor became interested in pop and rock musicians such as Carole King, Bruce Springsteen, and Madonna. She began to write some songs in these styles. Some people in the music world said Taylor's songs were good only because she had help from other songwriters. They believed she was too young to write great music on her own. Taylor was determined to prove them wrong. Her next two albums were *Speak Now* and *Red*. She wrote every song on them by herself. Her fans loved them. These new albums were a mix of country and pop. They attracted even more fans, both teens and adults.

Many **celebrities** like to keep a distance from their fans. But Taylor liked being close to hers. During concerts, she walked through the crowd. She happily signed **autographs**. She invited small groups of Swifties to watch her rehearse before big concerts. Sometimes she surprised fans by inviting other famous singers to perform in her shows.

Now a superstar, Taylor went on tour around the world. She broke records for ticket sales and won many awards for her music.

Taylor with fans **Mila Heisen** and **Juniper Schutz**.

To me, **fearless isn't not having fears...** I think that being fearless is having a lot of fears, but you **jump anyway.**

WHEN?

Taylor tours with other country singers.

Taylor releases *Fearless.*

Taylor headlines her first concert tour.

— **2007** ——— **2008** ——— **2009** —

Taylor wins four Grammy awards.

Taylor releases *Speak Now.*

Taylor releases *Red.*

— **2009** ——— **2010** ——— **2012** —

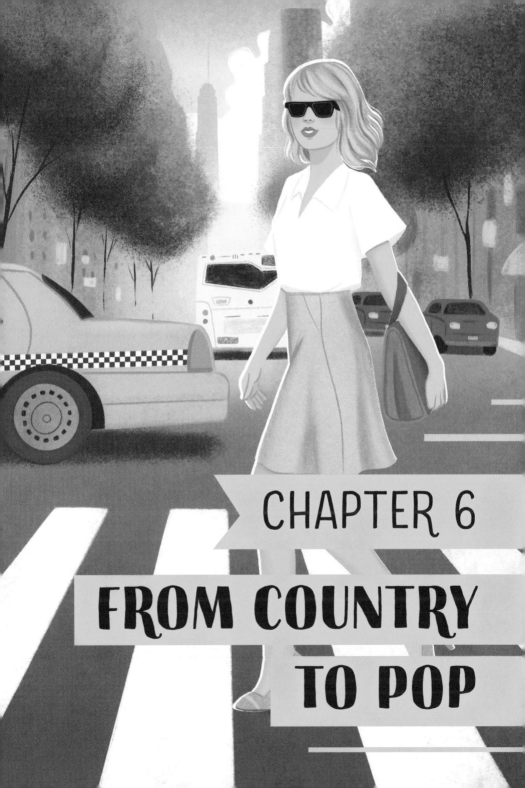

CHAPTER 6

FROM COUNTRY TO POP

🎵 Life in New York 🎵

In 2014, Taylor turned 25 years old. She wanted to write only pop music in order to reach more fans. So she left Nashville and moved to New York City. Her new apartment had ten bedrooms and ten bathrooms. She enjoyed the busy city life. When she wasn't working, she hung out with friends in her new home and shared cookies that she baked herself.

Taylor loves animals and got two special cats to keep her company in her big apartment. Meredith Grey, a shy cat, came with her from Nashville.

Meredith was named after a character from Taylor's favorite television show. Taylor adopted her kitten Olivia Benson shortly after moving to New York. Olivia was named after a detective on another show she liked. Taylor often shared photos of her cats on **social media**, and they even appeared in commercials and music videos with her.

That year, Taylor was working on her first pop album. It was called *1989*. Taylor wrote songs about her grown-up life and how she had changed since 1989, the year she was born.

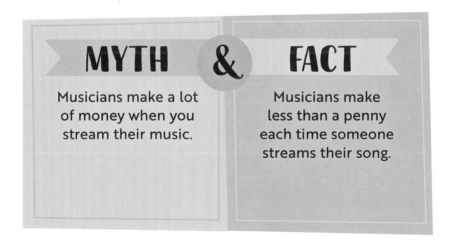

MYTH & FACT

Musicians make a lot of money when you stream their music.

Musicians make less than a penny each time someone streams their song.

The song "Shake It Off" was about not letting mean people get you down. "Blank Space" was a funny song about how people like to gossip about her love life.

Making a pop album was risky. Taylor was a country music star, but she wasn't sure she could be a pop star, too. Then *1989* went straight to number one on the Billboard 200 chart, and it stayed in the top ten for a year. Taylor was a pop star!

◎ Taking a Break ◎

As Taylor became more famous, she used her fame to help other musicians. More people were using **streaming services** to listen to music. Taylor didn't think streaming services were paying musicians fairly. She took a stand by taking her music off the streaming services until they made changes to how they paid musicians.

When Taylor felt she needed a break from
fame and performing, she stopped posting on
social media and did only a few shows. For a
year, she lived a quiet life, spent time with her
family, and wrote new songs. Then, in 2017,
she told her fans she had a new album. It was
called *Reputation*. Taylor was back, and she had

JUMP
—IN THE—
THINK
TANK

Taylor took time off when she needed a break. What do you do when you need a break? How do you relax?

changed again. She even rapped in some of her songs, such as "... Ready for It?" and "End Game." She still sang about boyfriends, but also about personal struggles. She wanted her fans to know the real her, not just what they read online or in magazines.

By now, Taylor was also known for making great music videos. They were set in interesting places, had cool costumes, and sometimes included animals (such as horses and her cats!). Taylor liked to leave secret messages, or **Easter eggs**, in her songs and videos. These messages were playful clues about the people her songs were about, or what her next song or album would be. It was a fun way to connect with her fans and get them excited about her music. Taylor was not only a great singer but also a clever storyteller!

WHERE?

NEW YORK CITY

NASHVILLE

TENNESSEE

WHEN?

Taylor moves to New York City.	Taylor releases *1989*	Taylor wins three Grammy Awards for *1989*.	Taylor releases *Reputation*.
2014	**2014**	**2016**	**2017**

CHAPTER 7

SPREADING KINDNESS

⦿ Special Surprises ⦿

A year after Taylor released *Reputation,* she left Big Machine Records. She had decided to join another record label, Republic Records. Her first album with her new label was called *Lover.* It became the best-selling album by a **solo artist** in 2019.

But then something bad happened in 2020. The COVID-19 **pandemic** made the whole world shut down. People were feeling sad and scared. Taylor had to cancel her concert tours.

JUMP
—IN THE—
THINK
TANK

A documentary film presents real events and facts. What would you want to tell people about your life in a documentary?

That year, Taylor surprised her fans with two new albums: *Folklore* and *Evermore*. They were different from her other albums. Taylor sang quieter songs that told stories from her imagination, not just her real life. *Folklore* won the Grammy Album of the Year award. Taylor was the first woman to win this award three times.

Swifties got another treat that year. Taylor released a **documentary** called *Miss Americana*. In the film, Taylor speaks honestly about not always feeling great about herself. She talks about being

42

brave when people try to bring you down or take credit for your hard work. She talks about how social media can be hurtful. Specifically, she says it's important to use your voice to stand up for yourself, for others, and for what you believe in.

After *Miss Americana,* Taylor used her voice in a new way. She began to make new recordings of the albums she made when she was with Big Machine Records. She called them "Taylor's Version." They became even more popular than the originals!

◎ Taylor's Era ◎

In 2022, Taylor released her tenth album, called *Midnights.* The next year, she started her biggest concert tour ever. It was called the Eras Tour, and it set a record by selling the most concert tickets in one day. Taylor sang songs from each of her ten albums, starting from her country music days. The concerts brought people together like a big family. Lyrics from her song "You're on Your Own Kid" even inspired fans to make and trade friendship bracelets at her shows.

Taylor knew that not everyone could come to her concerts, so she made a movie of the tour for more fans to enjoy. In less than a day, it became the best-selling concert tour movie in history!

Taylor has won more than 600 awards for her music, including 14 Grammy Awards and 23 Video Music Awards. She has even won awards for her fashion! Taylor's style has inspired her fans to create their own styles and express themselves through their clothes.

Taylor is a superstar who also believes in spreading kindness. She opened a music education center in Nashville. She donated money to help victims of tornadoes and floods who lost their homes. She has even helped fans pay for college and medical bills. Taylor speaks up for important things such as women's rights and artists' rights, and she encourages people to vote and make a difference.

Taylor has been rocking the music world since she started singing in Nashville. Through her music, she has connected with people and helped them to feel less alone. She's a superstar who truly cares about her fans, and her story continues to inspire those around her.

> **No matter what happens in life,** be good to people. Being good to people is a wonderful **legacy to leave behind.**

WHEN?

Taylor releases *Lover.*

2019

Miss Americana comes out.

2020

Taylor releases *Folklore* and *Evermore.*

2020

Taylor releases *Midnights.*

2022

Eras Tour begins.

2023

Taylor releases *The Tortured Poets Department.*

2024

CHAPTER 8

SO ... WHO IS
TAYLOR
SWIFT
?

Challenge Accepted!

Now that you know so much about Taylor's inspiring life and success, let's test your knowledge in this who, what, when, where, why, and how quiz. Feel free to look back in the text to find the answers if you need to, but try to remember first!

1 **Where was Taylor born?**
→ A West Reading, Pennsylvania
→ B New York City
→ C Nashville, Tennessee
→ D San Francisco, California

2 **What kind of music did Taylor's grandmother sing?**
→ A Rock and roll
→ B Jazz
→ C Country
→ D Opera

3 What is the name of the first song Taylor wrote when she was 12?

→ A "Our Song"

→ B "Fearless"

→ C "Lucky You"

→ D "Shake It Off"

4 Where was Taylor singing when Big Machine Records offered her a deal?

→ A The Bluebird Cafe

→ B At a basketball game

→ C At a music producer's office

→ D In a school play

5 Who helped Taylor become a better songwriter?

→ A Marjorie Finley

→ B Liz Rose

→ C Dolly Parton

→ D Scott Borchetta

6 **What was the name of Taylor's first album?**

→ A Big Machine

→ B Taylor Swift

→ C 1989

→ D Tim McGraw

7 **Where did Taylor move to from Nashville?**

→ A New York City

→ B Philadelphia

→ C Music Row

→ D Paris

8 **What kind of pets does Taylor have?**

→ A Dogs

→ B Cats

→ C Horses

→ D Parrots

9 Why did Taylor remove her songs from music streaming services?

→ A   They were mean to her.

→ B   She needed a break from performing.

→ C   She wanted musical artists to be paid more fairly.

→ D   She preferred to make music videos.

10 What are Taylor's secret messages called?

→ A   Christmas trees

→ B   Candy canes

→ C   Scrambled eggs

→ D   Easter eggs

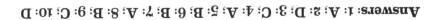

 Our World

Taylor Swift is one of the most popular singer-songwriters of our time. Let's look at some of the ways her accomplishments have helped shape our world today.

→ Everyone experiences times when they are sad, angry, or lonely. Some people handle these challenges in ways that hurt themselves or others. Taylor used her music to express her feelings. She is an example of how music, art, and other activities can help people deal with problems in positive ways.

→ Children and teens are often not taken seriously when they want to accomplish something big. When Taylor started out, no one in the music world believed in her. But she refused to give up. Taylor is an example of how you can achieve great things even when you are young.

→ There are many ways that people can be role models. Some help others and keep people safe, such as teachers, firefighters, and nurses. Others pave the way to freedom and human rights. Taylor is a role model because she has used her voice to make others feel heard and cared for while also sharing her wealth to help people in need.

JUMP —IN THE— THINK TANK FOR

⟩ MORE! ⟨

Let's think a little more about what Taylor Swift has done and how her success has affected the world we live in.

→ How does Taylor's story encourage you to follow your dreams?

→ Taylor helps others by giving back to her community. How can you help others?

→ Taylor took risks by trying new kinds of music. In what ways can it be scary to try new things?

Glossary

album: a collection of songs

autograph: a person's handwritten signature

Billboard charts: rankings of the week's most popular songs and albums based on sales

career: the job a person has for a long period of time

CD: short for compact disc, a small plastic disc on which music or other information is recorded

celebrity: a famous person

chord: three or more musical notes played at the same time

concert: a performance of music in front of an audience

contract: a written agreement between an artist and a record company

country music: also called country and western; a style of music that often tells stories about the lives of people in rural areas

documentary: a film that shows real facts and events and often includes short videos of the events as they happened

Easter eggs: surprises or coded messages hidden in books, music, videos, video games, or movies

Grammy: an award given to musicians for the best music each year

homeschool: to get an education at home instead of in a school

inspire: to give someone the feeling or desire to do something

lyrics: the words to a song

music producer: a person who assists musical artists with their recording projects and helps fund them

music video: a short film of a song, usually including dancing and images related to the lyrics

opera: a play in which all or most of the words are sung

pandemic: an outbreak of disease that spreads around the world and makes many people sick in a short period of time

perform: to entertain an audience

pop: short for popular music that is the most listened to and played on the radio

promote: to encourage people to like, buy, use, do, or support something

record label: a company that works with musicians to make and sell music

singer-songwriter: a performer who writes songs and sings them

social media: websites and other applications that enable users to create and share content

solo artist: a performer who sings by him- or herself, rather than as part of a musical group

streaming service: a web-based service that lets users listen to songs on their computers or mobile devices

studio: a place where audio recordings are made

tour: a series of concerts by an artist or group of artists in different cities, countries, or locations

Bibliography

Books

Kawa, Katie. *Taylor Swift: Making a Difference as a Songwriter*. New York: KidHaven Publishing, 2022.

Kawa, Katie. *Taylor Swift: Superstar Singer*. New York: Lucent Press, 2017.

Schwartz, Heather E. *Taylor Swift: Superstar Singer and Songwriter*. Minneapolis: Lerner Publications, 2019.

Websites

Taylor Swift Vevo
youtube.com/user/taylorswiftvevo
Official YouTube page for Swift's music videos and behind-the-scenes video content

Taylor Swift Museum
theswiftmuseum.com

Songfacts
songfacts.com/facts/taylor-swift

Billboard
billboard.com/artist/taylor-swift/

Grammy Awards: Taylor Swift
grammy.com/artists/taylor-swift/15450

About the Author

 **Rachelle Burk** writes fiction and nonfiction for children ages 2 to 13. Her other Callisto Kids titles include *The Story of Simone Biles, Stomp, Wiggle, Clap, and Tap: My First Book of Dance, Women Who Changed the World,* and *Let's Play an Instrument: A Music Book for Kids.* Other picture books include *Don't Turn the Page!, A Mitzvah for George Washington,* and *A Gift of Life: A Story of Organ and Tissue Donation.* Rachelle's middle grade science adventure novel, *The Walking Fish,* is a National Science Teaching Association award winner. She loves to visit schools around the country. You can find out more about her books and author visits at RachelleBurk.com.

About the Illustrator

Marta Dorado is a full-time freelance illustrator born in Gijón (Asturias, Spain) in 1989 and raised in a nearby village. She attended university in Pamplona, where she still lives, and started a career as a graphic designer in the advertising industry. Marta's childhood, surrounded by nature and close to the sea, strongly influences her work.

WHO WILL INSPIRE YOU NEXT?

EXPLORE A WORLD OF HEROES AND ROLE MODELS IN **THE STORY OF** ...AN INSPIRING BIOGRAPHY SERIES FOR YOUNG READERS.

THE STORY OF
PRINCESS DIANA
AN INSPIRING BIOGRAPHY FOR YOUNG READERS
JENNA GRODZICKI

THE STORY OF
MISTY COPELAND
AN INSPIRING BIOGRAPHY FOR YOUNG READERS
FRANK BERRIOS

THE STORY OF
ELLA FITZGERALD
AN INSPIRING BIOGRAPHY FOR YOUNG READERS
KATHY TRUSTY

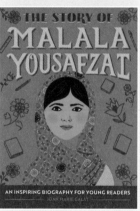

THE STORY OF
MALALA YOUSAFZAI
AN INSPIRING BIOGRAPHY FOR YOUNG READERS
JOAN MARIE GALAT

LOOK FOR THIS SERIES
WHEREVER BOOKS AND EBOOKS ARE SOLD